MW00912337

BOOK ONE

# DISCOVERING

ANCIENT

# WISDOM

*Practical Words of Insight and Understanding*

ZondervanPublishingHouse
*Grand Rapids, Michigan*

*A Division of HarperCollinsPublishers*

Discovering Ancient Wisdom, Book One -
Practical Words of Insight and Understanding
© 1995 by IBS Publishing

🏛 Zondervan Publishing House
5300 Patterson Ave., S.E.
Grand Rapids, Michigan 49530

Selections from Proverbs from the NIV
Printed in U.S.A.
ISBN:0-310-96351-6                                    8/95

*Where then does wisdom come from?*
*Where does understanding*
*dwell?*

# Reading one

*Wisdom is supreme; therefore get wisdom.*
  *Though it cost all you have, get understanding.*
*Esteem her, and she will exalt you;*
  *embrace her, and she will honor you.*
*She will set a garland of grace on your head*
  *and present you with a crown of splendor.*

*Listen, my son, accept what I say,*
  *and the years of your life will be many.*
*I guide you in the way of wisdom*
  *and lead you along straight paths.*
*When you walk, your steps will not be hampered;*
  *when you run, you will not stumble.*

*Hold on to instruction, do not let it go;*
  *guard it well, for it is your life.*

Do not set foot on the path of the wicked
  or walk in the way of evil men.
Avoid it, do not travel on it;
  turn from it and go on your way.
They eat the bread of wickedness
  and drink the wine of violence.

Above all else, guard your heart,
  for it is the wellspring of life.
Put away perversity from your mouth;
  keep corrupt talk far from your lips.
Make level paths for your feet
  and take only ways that are firm.
Do not swerve to the right or the left;
  keep your foot from evil.

Do not forsake wisdom, and she will protect you;
  love her, and she will watch over you.

# Reading two

*Blessed is the man who finds wisdom,*
  *the man who gains understanding,*
*for she is more profitable than silver*
  *and yields better returns than gold.*
*She is more precious than rubies;*
  *nothing you desire can compare with her.*
*Long life is in her right hand;*
  *in her left hand are riches and honor.*
*Her ways are pleasant ways,*
  *and all her paths are peace.*
*She is a tree of life to those who embrace her;*
  *those who lay hold of her will be blessed.*

*Let love and faithfulness never leave you;*
  *bind them around your neck,*
  *write them on the tablet of your heart.*

My son, preserve sound judgment and discernment,
  do not let them out of your sight;
they will be life for you,
  an ornament to grace your neck.
Then you will go on your way in safety,
  and your foot will not stumble;
when you lie down, you will not be afraid;
  when you lie down, your sleep will be sweet.

Do not plot harm against your neighbor,
  who lives trustfully near you.

Do not accuse a man for no reason—
  when he has done you no harm.

Do not withhold good from those who deserve it,
  when it is in your power to act.

# Reading three

Do not boast about tomorrow,
   for you do not know what a day may bring forth.

Let another praise you, and not your own mouth;
   someone else, and not your own lips.

Stone is heavy and sand a burden,
   but provocation by a fool is heavier than both.

Anger is cruel and fury overwhelming,
   but who can stand before jealousy?

Better is open rebuke than hidden love.

Wounds from a friend can be trusted,
   but an enemy multiplies kisses.

Like a bird that strays from its nest
   is a man who strays from his home.

Perfume and incense bring joy to the heart,
   and the pleasantness of one's friend
      springs from his earnest counsel.

The prudent see danger and take refuge,
   but the simple keep going and suffer for it.

If a man loudly blesses his neighbor early in the
   morning, it will be taken as a curse.

As iron sharpens iron, so one man sharpens another.

He who tends a fig tree will eat its fruit,
   and he who looks after his master will be honored.

Death and Destruction are never satisfied,
   and neither are the eyes of man.

The crucible for silver and the furnace for gold,
   but man is tested by the praise he receives.

# Reading four

*When pride comes, then comes disgrace,*
*    but with humility comes wisdom.*

*The integrity of the upright guides them,*
*    but the unfaithful are destroyed by their duplicity.*

*The righteousness of the upright delivers them,*
*    but the unfaithful are trapped by evil desires.*

*A man who lacks judgment derides his neighbor,*
*    but a man of understanding holds his tongue.*

*A gossip betrays a confidence,*
*    but a trustworthy man keeps a secret.*

*He who puts up security for another will surely suffer,*
*    but whoever refuses to strike hands in pledge is safe.*

*The LORD detests men of perverse heart*
*    but he delights in those whose ways are blameless.*

Be sure of this: The wicked will not go unpunished,
   but those who are righteous will go free.

Like a gold ring in a pig's snout
   is a beautiful woman who shows no discretion.

One man gives freely, yet gains even more;
   another withholds unduly, but comes to poverty.

A generous man will prosper;
   he who refreshes others will himself be refreshed.

He who seeks good finds goodwill,
   but evil comes to him who searches for it.

Whoever trusts in his riches will fall,
   but the righteous will thrive like a green leaf.

He who brings trouble on his family
   will inherit only wind,
   and the fool will be servant to the wise.

# Reading five

*Do you see a man wise in his own eyes?*
  *There is more hope for a fool than for him.*

*Do not answer a fool according to his folly,*
  *or you will be like him yourself.*

*Like a fluttering sparrow or a darting swallow,*
  *an undeserved curse does not come to rest.*

*Like cutting off one's feet or drinking violence*
  *is the sending of a message by the hand of a fool.*

*Like a lame man's legs that hang limp*
  *is a proverb in the mouth of a fool.*

*Like an archer who wounds at random*
  *is he who hires a fool or any passer-by.*

*Like one who seizes a dog by the ears*
  *is a passer-by who meddles in a quarrel not his own.*

Like a madman shooting firebrands or deadly
  arrows is a man who deceives his neighbor
  and says, "I was only joking!"

Without wood a fire goes out;
  without gossip a quarrel dies down.

As charcoal to embers and as wood to fire,
  so is a quarrelsome man for kindling strife.

The words of a gossip are like choice morsels;
  they go down to a man's inmost parts.

Like a coating of glaze over earthenware
  are fervent lips with an evil heart.

A malicious man disguises himself with his lips,
  but in his heart he harbors deceit.
Though his speech is charming,
  do not believe him.

# Reading six

*Pride goes before destruction, a haughty spirit before a fall.*

*How much better to get wisdom than gold,*
  *to choose understanding rather than silver!*

*All a man's ways seem innocent to him,*
  *but motives are weighed by the LORD.*

*Better a little with righteousness*
  *than much gain with injustice.*

*Kings detest wrongdoing,*
  *for a throne is established through righteousness.*

*The highway of the upright avoids evil;*
  *he who guards his way guards his life.*

*Better to be lowly in spirit and among the oppressed*
  *than to share plunder with the proud.*

The wise in heart are called discerning,
  and pleasant words promote instruction.

Understanding is a fountain of life to those who have it,
  but folly brings punishment to fools.

Pleasant words are a honeycomb,
  sweet to the soul and healing to the bones.

There is a way that seems right to a man,
  but in the end it leads to death.

A scoundrel plots evil,
  and his speech is like a scorching fire.

A perverse man stirs up dissension,
  and a gossip separates close friends.

A wise man's heart guides his mouth,
  and his lips promote instruction.

# Reading seven

*A word aptly spoken is like apples of gold in settings of silve*

*Do not exalt yourself in the king's presence,*
  *and do not claim a place among great men;*
*it is better for him to say to you, "Come up here,"*
  *than for him to humiliate you before a nobleman.*

*If you argue your case with a neighbor,*
  *do not betray another man's confidence,*
*or he who hears it may shame you*
  *and you will never lose your bad reputation.*

*Like an earring of gold or an ornament of fine gold*
  *is a wise man's rebuke to a listening ear.*

*Like the coolness of snow at harvest time*
  *is a trustworthy messenger to those who send him;*
  *he refreshes the spirit of his masters.*

*Like clouds and wind without rain*
*is a man who boasts of gifts he does not give.*

*Seldom set foot in your neighbor's house—*
*too much of you, and he will hate you.*

*Like a bad tooth or a lame foot*
*is reliance on the unfaithful in times of trouble.*

*As a north wind brings rain,*
*so a sly tongue brings angry looks.*

*It is not good to eat too much honey,*
*nor is it honorable to seek one's own honor.*

*Like a city whose walls are broken down*
*is a man who lacks self-control.*

*If your enemy is hungry, give him food to eat;*
*if he is thirsty, give him water to drink.*

# eading eight

*Wisdom calls aloud in the street,*
  *she raises her voice in the public squares;*
*at the head of the noisy streets she cries out,*
  *in the gateways of the city she makes her speech:*

*"How long will you simple ones love your simple ways?*
  *How long will mockers delight in mockery*
    *and fools hate knowledge?*
*If you had responded to my rebuke,*
  *I would have poured out my heart to you*
    *and made my thoughts known to you.*
*But since you rejected me when I called*
  *and no one gave heed when I stretched out my hand,*
*since you ignored all my advice*
  *and would not accept my rebuke,*
*I in turn will laugh at your disaster;*

*I will mock when calamity overtakes you—*
   *when calamity overtakes you like a storm,*
*when disaster sweeps over you like a whirlwind,*
   *when distress and trouble overwhelm you.*

*"Then they will call to me but I will not answer;*
   *they will look for me but will not find me.*
*Since they hated knowledge*
   *and did not choose to fear the LORD,*
*since they would not accept my advice*
   *and spurned my rebuke,*
*they will eat the fruit of their ways*
   *and be filled with the fruit of their schemes.*
*For the waywardness of the simple will kill them,*
   *and the complacency of fools will destroy them;*
*but whoever listens to me will live in safety*
   *and be at ease,*
   *without fear of harm."*

# Reading nine

It is not good to have zeal without knowledge,
    nor to be hasty and miss the way.

He who gets wisdom loves his own soul;
    he who cherishes understanding prospers.

A false witness will not go unpunished,
    and he who pours out lies will perish.

A man's wisdom gives him patience;
    it is to his glory to overlook an offense.

A king's rage is like the roar of a lion,
    but his favor is like dew on the grass.

A foolish son is his father's ruin,
    and a quarrelsome wife is like a constant dripping.

He who is kind to the poor lends to the LORD,
    and he will reward him for what he has done.

*Discipline your son, for in that there is hope;*
  *do not be a willing party to his death.*

*A hot-tempered man must pay the penalty;*
  *if you rescue him, you will have to do it again.*

*He who robs his father and drives out his mother*
  *is a son who brings shame and disgrace.*

*A corrupt witness mocks at justice,*
  *and the mouth of the wicked gulps down evil.*

*Stop listening to instruction, my son,*
  *and you will stray from the words of knowledge.*

*Listen to advice and accept instruction,*
  *and in the end you will be wise.*

*Many are the plans in a man's heart,*
  *but it is the LORD's purpose that prevails.*

# Reading ten

Better a poor man whose walk is blameless
   than a rich man whose ways are perverse.

The wicked man flees though no one pursues,
   but the righteous are as bold as a lion.

When a country is rebellious, it has many rulers,
   but a man of understanding and knowledge maintains ord

Those who forsake the law praise the wicked,
   but those who keep the law resist them.

A rich man may be wise in his own eyes,
   but a poor man who has discernment sees through him.

When the righteous triumph, there is great elation;
   but when the wicked rise to power, men go into hiding.

A man tormented by the guilt of murder
   will be a fugitive till death; let no one support him.

*He whose walk is blameless is kept safe,*
  *but he whose ways are perverse will suddenly fall.*

*He who works his land will have abundant food,*
  *but the one who chases fantasies*
  *will have his fill of poverty.*

*A stingy man is eager to get rich*
  *and is unaware that poverty awaits him.*

*He who robs his father or mother*
  *and says, "It's not wrong"—*
  *he is partner to him who destroys.*

*He who gives to the poor will lack nothing,*
  *but he who closes his eyes to them*
  *receives many curses.*

*He who trusts in himself is a fool,*
  *but he who walks in wisdom is kept safe.*

# Reading eleven

A heart at peace gives life to the body,
  but envy rots the bones.

The mocker seeks wisdom and finds none,
  but knowledge comes easily to the discerning.

Fools mock at making amends for sin,
  but goodwill is found among the upright.

Stay away from a foolish man,
  for you will not find knowledge on his lips.

The house of the wicked will be destroyed,
  but the tent of the upright will flourish.

The faithless will be fully repaid for their ways,
  and the good man rewarded for his.

A quick-tempered man does foolish things,
  and a crafty man is hated.

He who despises his neighbor sins,
  but blessed is he who is kind to the needy.

Do not those who plot evil go astray?
  But those who plan what is good find love
  and faithfulness.

A patient man has great understanding,
  but a quick-tempered man displays folly.

The wise woman builds her house,
  but with her own hands the foolish one tears hers down.

He who oppresses the poor shows contempt for their Maker,
  but whoever is kind to the needy honors God.

When a calamity comes, the wicked are brought down,
  but even in death the righteous have a refuge.

Righteousness exalts a nation,
  but sin is a disgrace to any people.

# Reading twelve

Listen, my son, to your father's instruction
   and do not forsake your mother's teaching.
They will be a garland to grace your head
   and a chain to adorn your neck.

My son, if sinners entice you,
   do not give in to them.
If they say, "Come along with us;
   let's lie in wait for someone's blood,
   let's waylay some harmless soul;
let's swallow them alive, like the grave,
   and whole, like those who go down to the pit;
we will get all sorts of valuable things
   and fill our houses with plunder;
throw in your lot with us,
   and we will share a common purse"—

*my son, do not go along with them,*
*    do not set foot on their paths;*
*for their feet rush into sin,*
*    they are swift to shed blood.*

*How useless to spread a net*
*    in full view of all the birds!*
*These men lie in wait for their own blood;*
*    they waylay only themselves!*
*Such is the end of all who go after ill-gotten gain;*
*    it takes away the lives of those who get it.*

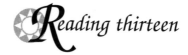

# Reading thirteen

A fortune made by a lying tongue
  is a fleeting vapor and a deadly snare.

The plans of the diligent lead to profit
  as surely as haste leads to poverty.

The violence of the wicked will drag them away,
  for they refuse to do what is right.

The way of the guilty is devious,
  but the conduct of the innocent is upright.

The wicked man craves evil;
  his neighbor gets no mercy from him.

If a man shuts his ears to the cry of the poor,
  he too will cry out and not be answered.

When justice is done, it brings joy to the righteous
  but terror to evildoers.

28

A man who strays from the path of understanding
  comes to rest in the company of the dead.

He who loves pleasure will become poor;
  whoever loves wine and oil will never be rich.

In the house of the wise are stores of choice food and oil,
  but a foolish man devours all he has.

He who pursues righteousness and love
  finds life, prosperity and honor.

He who guards his mouth and his tongue
  keeps himself from calamity.

The proud and arrogant man— "Mocker" is his name;
  he behaves with overweening pride.

There is no wisdom, no insight, no plan
  that can succeed against the LORD.

# Reading fourteen

*Does not wisdom call out?*
  *Does not understanding raise her voice?*

*Choose my instruction instead of silver,*
  *knowledge rather than choice gold,*
*for wisdom is more precious than rubies,*
  *and nothing you desire can compare with her.*
*By me kings reign*
  *and rulers make laws that are just;*
*by me princes govern,*
  *and all nobles who rule on earth.*

*I love those who love me,*
  *and those who seek me find me.*
*My fruit is better than fine gold;*
  *what I yield surpasses choice silver.*

*I walk in the way of righteousness,*
  *along the paths of justice,*
*bestowing wealth on those who love me*
  *and making their treasuries full.*

*The LORD brought me forth as the first of his works,*
  *before his deeds of old;*
*I was appointed from eternity,*
  *from the beginning, before the world began.*
*When there were no oceans, I was given birth,*
  *when there were no springs abounding with water;*
*before the mountains were settled in place,*
  *before the hills, I was given birth,*
*before he made the earth or its fields*
  *or any of the dust of the world.*

*Listen to my instruction and be wise;*
  *do not ignore it.*

# Reading fifteen

A fool gives full vent to his anger,
   but a wise man keeps himself under control.

A man who remains stiff-necked after many rebukes
   will suddenly be destroyed—without remedy.

By justice a king gives a country stability,
   but one who is greedy for bribes tears it down.

A man who loves wisdom brings joy to his father,
   but a companion of prostitutes squanders his wealth.

The righteous care about justice for the poor,
   but the wicked have no such concern.

Mockers stir up a city,
   but wise men turn away anger.

Bloodthirsty men hate a man of integrity
   and seek to kill the upright.

If a ruler listens to lies,
all his officials become wicked.

If a king judges the poor with fairness,
his throne will always be secure.

Discipline your son, and he will give you peace;
he will bring delight to your soul.

Where there is no revelation, the people cast off restraint;
but blessed is he who keeps the law.

Do you see a man who speaks in haste?
There is more hope for a fool than for him.

An angry man stirs up dissension,
and a hot-tempered one commits many sins.

Many seek an audience with a ruler,
but it is from the LORD that man gets justice.

*Do not envy wicked men, do not desire their company.*

*Rescue those being led away to death;*
  *hold back those staggering toward slaughter.*

*Do not lie in wait like an outlaw*
  *against a righteous man's house,*
  *do not raid his dwelling place;*
*for though a righteous man falls seven times, he rises again,*
  *but the wicked are brought down by calamity.*

*Do not gloat when your enemy falls;*
  *when he stumbles, do not let your heart rejoice.*

*To show partiality in judging is not good.*

*Do not say, "I'll do to him as he has done to me;*
  *I'll pay that man back for what he did."*

An honest answer is like a kiss on the lips.

A little sleep, a little slumber,
   a little folding of the hands to rest—
and poverty will come on you like a bandit
   and scarcity like an armed man.

Whoever says to the guilty, "You are innocent"—
   peoples will curse him and nations denounce him.
But it will go well with those who convict the guilty,
   and rich blessing will come upon them.

Do not testify against your neighbor without cause,
   or use your lips to deceive.

Do not fret because of evil men
   or be envious of the wicked,
for the evil man has no future hope,
   and the lamp of the wicked will be snuffed out.

# 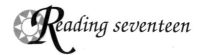Reading seventeen

Gold there is, and rubies in abundance,
  but lips that speak knowledge are a rare jewel.

Many a man claims to have unfailing love,
  but a faithful man who can find?

Do not love sleep or you will grow poor;
  stay awake and you will have food to spare.

Wine is a mocker and beer a brawler;
  whoever is led astray by them is not wise.

It is to a man's honor to avoid strife,
  but every fool is quick to quarrel.

Even a child is known by his actions,
  by whether his conduct is pure and right.

"It's no good, it's no good!" says the buyer;
  then off he goes and boasts about his purchase.

*Food gained by fraud tastes sweet to a man,*
  *but he ends up with a mouth full of gravel.*

*A gossip betrays a confidence;*
  *so avoid a man who talks too much.*

*If a man curses his father or mother,*
  *his lamp will be snuffed out in pitch darkness.*

*An inheritance quickly gained at the beginning*
  *will not be blessed at the end.*

*Do not say, "I'll pay you back for this wrong!"*
  *Wait for the LORD, and he will deliver you.*

*The glory of young men is their strength,*
  *gray hair the splendor of the old.*

*The purposes of a man's heart are deep waters,*
  *but a man of understanding draws them out.*

# Reading eighteen

Listen to your father, who gave you life,
   and do not despise your mother when she is old.
Listen, my son, and be wise,
   and keep your heart on the right path.
Do not join those who drink too much wine
   or gorge themselves on meat,
for drunkards and gluttons become poor,
   and drowsiness clothes them in rags.

Do not eat the food of a stingy man,
   do not crave his delicacies;
for he is the kind of man
   who is always thinking about the cost.
"Eat and drink," he says to you,
   but his heart is not with you.

*Who has woe? Who has sorrow?*
  *Who has strife? Who has complaints?*
  *Who has needless bruises? Who has bloodshot eyes?*
*Those who linger over wine,*
  *who go to sample bowls of mixed wine.*
*Do not gaze at wine when it is red,*
  *when it sparkles in the cup,*
  *when it goes down smoothly!*

*In the end it bites like a snake*
  *and poisons like a viper.*
*Your eyes will see strange sights*
  *and your mind imagine confusing things.*
*You will be like one sleeping on the high seas,*
  *lying on top of the rigging.*
*"They hit me," you will say, "but I'm not hurt!*
  *They beat me, but I don't feel it!*
*When will I wake up*
  *so I can find another drink?"*

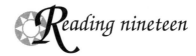

# Reading nineteen

A gentle answer turns away wrath,
  but a harsh word stirs up anger.

A hot-tempered man stirs up dissension,
  but a patient man calms a quarrel.

The tongue that brings healing is a tree of life,
  but a deceitful tongue crushes the spirit.

Stern discipline awaits him who leaves the path;
  he who hates correction will die.

A mocker resents correction;
  he will not consult the wise.

The discerning heart seeks knowledge,
  but the mouth of a fool feeds on folly.

Better a meal of vegetables where there is love
  than a fattened calf with hatred.

A wise son brings joy to his father,
    but a foolish man despises his mother.

Plans fail for lack of counsel,
    but with many advisers they succeed.

The LORD tears down the proud man's house
    but he keeps the widow's boundaries intact.

A greedy man brings trouble to his family,
    but he who hates bribes will live.

The heart of the righteous weighs its answers,
    but the mouth of the wicked gushes evil.

He who listens to a life-giving rebuke
    will be at home among the wise.

He who ignores discipline despises himself,
    but whoever heeds correction gains understanding.

# Reading twenty

*When words are many, sin is not absent,*
  *but he who holds his tongue is wise.*

*The wise in heart accept commands,*
  *but a chattering fool comes to ruin.*

*The man of integrity walks securely,*
  *but he who takes crooked paths will be found out.*

*Ill-gotten treasures are of no value,*
  *but righteousness delivers from death.*

*Lazy hands make a man poor,*
  *but diligent hands bring wealth.*

*Hatred stirs up dissension,*
  *but love covers over all wrongs.*

*He who heeds discipline shows the way to life,*
  *but whoever ignores correction leads others astray.*

*He who conceals his hatred has lying lips,*
  *and whoever spreads slander is a fool.*

*The lips of the righteous nourish many,*
  *but fools die for lack of judgment.*

*A fool finds pleasure in evil conduct,*
  *but a man of understanding delights in wisdom.*

*The fear of the LORD adds length to life,*
  *but the years of the wicked are cut short.*

*What the wicked dreads will overtake him;*
  *what the righteous desire will be granted.*

*When the storm has swept by, the wicked are gone,*
  *but the righteous stand firm forever.*

*The prospect of the righteous is joy,*
  *but the hopes of the wicked come to nothing.*

# Reading twenty-one

One who is slack in his work
  is brother to one who destroys.

An unfriendly man pursues selfish ends;
  he defies all sound judgment.

A fool finds no pleasure in understanding
  but delights in airing his own opinions.

It is not good to be partial to the wicked
  or to deprive the innocent of justice.

A fool's mouth is his undoing,
  and his lips are a snare to his soul.

The wealth of the rich is their fortified city;
  they imagine it an unscalable wall.

Before his downfall a man's heart is proud,
  but humility comes before honor.

He who answers before listening—
  that is his folly and his shame.

A man's spirit sustains him in sickness,
  but a crushed spirit who can bear?

The heart of the discerning acquires knowledge;
  the ears of the wise seek it out.

The first to present his case seems right,
  till another comes forward and questions him.

An offended brother is more unyielding
  than a fortified city,
    and disputes are like the barred gates of a citadel.

He who finds a wife finds what is good
  and receives favor from the LORD.

A man of many companions may come to ruin,
  but there is a friend who sticks closer than a brother.

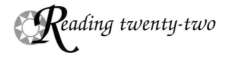

# Reading twenty-two

*Who has gone up to heaven and come down?*
  *Who has gathered up the wind in the hollow of his hands?*
*Who has wrapped up the waters in his cloak?*
  *Who has established all the ends of the earth?*
*What is his name, and the name of his son?*
  *Tell me if you know!*

*Two things I ask of you, O LORD;*
  *do not refuse me before I die:*
*Keep falsehood and lies far from me;*
  *give me neither poverty nor riches,*
  *but give me only my daily bread.*
*Otherwise, I may have too much and disown you*
  *and say, "Who is the LORD?"*
*Or I may become poor and steal,*
  *and so dishonor the name of my God.*

The eye that mocks a father,
  that scorns obedience to a mother,
will be pecked out by the ravens of the valley,
  will be eaten by the vultures.

This is the way of an adulteress:
  She eats and wipes her mouth and says,
  "I've done nothing wrong."

Under three things the earth trembles,
  under four it cannot bear up:
a servant who becomes king,
  a fool who is full of food,
an unloved woman who is married,
  and a maidservant who displaces her mistress.

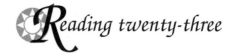
# Reading twenty-three

He who guards his lips guards his life,
  but he who speaks rashly will come to ruin.

The sluggard craves and gets nothing,
  but the desires of the diligent are fully satisfied.

One man pretends to be rich, yet has nothing;
  another pretends to be poor, yet has great wealth.

A man's riches may ransom his life,
  but a poor man hears no threat.

The light of the righteous shines brightly,
  but the lamp of the wicked is snuffed out.

Pride only breeds quarrels,
  but wisdom is found in those who take advice.

Dishonest money dwindles away,
  but he who gathers money little by little makes it grow.

48

*Hope deferred makes the heart sick,*
  *but a longing fulfilled is a tree of life.*

*He who scorns instruction will pay for it,*
  *but he who respects a command is rewarded.*

*The teaching of the wise is a fountain of life,*
  *turning a man from the snares of death.*

*He who ignores discipline comes to poverty and shame,*
  *but whoever heeds correction is honored.*

*A longing fulfilled is sweet to the soul,*
  *but fools detest turning from evil.*

*He who spares the rod hates his son,*
  *but he who loves him is careful to discipline him.*

*He who walks with the wise grows wise,*
  *but a companion of fools suffers harm.*

# Reading twenty-four

A wife of noble character who can find?
  She is worth far more than rubies.

She is clothed with strength and dignity;
  she can laugh at the days to come.
She watches over the affairs of her household
  and does not eat the bread of idleness.
When it snows, she has no fear for her household;
  for all of them are clothed in scarlet.
She makes linen garments and sells them,
  and supplies the merchants with sashes.
Her children arise and call her blessed;
  her husband also, and he praises her.
Many women do noble things,
  but you surpass them all.

*Her husband has full confidence in her*
  *and lacks nothing of value.*
*She considers a field and buys it;*
  *out of her earnings she plants a vineyard.*
*She sets about her work vigorously;*
  *her arms are strong for her tasks.*
*She sees that her trading is profitable,*
  *and her lamp does not go out at night.*
*She opens her arms to the poor*
  *and extends her hands to the needy.*

*She speaks with wisdom,*
  *and faithful instruction is on her tongue.*
*Charm is deceptive, and beauty is fleeting;*
  *but a woman who fears the LORD is to be praised.*
*Give her the reward she has earned,*
  *and let her works bring her praise at the city gate.*

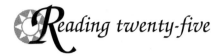

# Reading twenty-five

A good name is more desirable than great riches;
    to be esteemed is better than silver or gold.

A prudent man sees danger and takes refuge,
    but the simple keep going and suffer for it.

Train a child in the way he should go,
    and when he is old he will not turn from it.

The rich rule over the poor,
    and the borrower is servant to the lender.

Rich and poor have this in common:
    The LORD is the Maker of them all.

In the paths of the wicked lie thorns and snares,
    but he who guards his soul stays far from them.

He who sows wickedness reaps trouble,
    and the rod of his fury will be destroyed.

Drive out the mocker, and out goes strife;
  quarrels and insults are ended.

He who oppresses the poor to increase his wealth
  and he who gives gifts to the rich—
  both come to poverty.

Do not exploit the poor because they are poor
  and do not crush the needy in court,
for the LORD will take up their case
  and will plunder those who plunder them.

Do not make friends with a hot-tempered man,
  do not associate with one easily angered,
or you may learn his ways
  and get yourself ensnared.

Do not be a man who strikes hands in pledge
  or puts up security for debts;
if you lack the means to pay,
  your very bed will be snatched from under you.

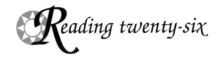
# Reading twenty-six

Truthful lips endure forever,
  but a lying tongue lasts only a moment.

A fool shows his annoyance at once,
  but a prudent man overlooks an insult.

A man cannot be established through wickedness,
  but the righteous cannot be uprooted.

Wicked men are overthrown and are no more,
  but the house of the righteous stands firm.

A wife of noble character is her husband's crown,
  but a disgraceful wife is like decay in his bones.

The plans of the righteous are just,
  but the advice of the wicked is deceitful.

A man is praised according to his wisdom,
  but men with warped minds are despised.

*He who works his land will have abundant food,*
*but he who chases fantasies lacks judgment.*

*Better to be a nobody and yet have a servant*
*than pretend to be somebody and have no food.*

*A righteous man cares for the needs of his animal,*
*but the kindest acts of the wicked are cruel.*

*An evil man is trapped by his sinful talk,*
*but a righteous man escapes trouble.*

*From the fruit of his lips a man is filled with good things*
*as surely as the work of his hands rewards him.*

*The way of a fool seems right to him,*
*but a wise man listens to advice.*

*Reckless words pierce like a sword,*
*but the tongue of the wise brings healing.*

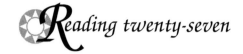

*Better a dry crust with peace and quiet*
*than a house full of feasting, with strife.*

*He who mocks the poor shows contempt for their Maker;*
*whoever gloats over disaster will not go unpunished.*

*Children's children are a crown to the aged,*
*and parents are the pride of their children.*

*Arrogant lips are unsuited to a fool—*
*how much worse lying lips to a ruler!*

*He who covers over an offense promotes love,*
*but whoever repeats the matter separates close friends.*

*An evil man is bent only on rebellion;*
*a merciless official will be sent against him.*

*If a man pays back evil for good,*
*evil will never leave his house.*

*A friend loves at all times,*
  *and a brother is born for adversity.*

*He who loves a quarrel loves sin;*
  *he who builds a high gate invites destruction.*

*A man of perverse heart does not prosper;*
  *he whose tongue is deceitful falls into trouble.*

*A cheerful heart is good medicine,*
  *but a crushed spirit dries up the bones.*

*A foolish son brings grief to his father*
  *and bitterness to the one who bore him.*

*A man of knowledge uses words with restraint,*
  *and a man of understanding is even-tempered.*

*Even a fool is thought wise if he keeps silent,*
  *and discerning if he holds his tongue.*

# Reading twenty-eight

*Wisdom has built her house;*
  *she has hewn out its seven pillars.*
*She has prepared her meat and mixed her wine;*
  *she has also set her table.*
*She has sent out her maids,*
  *and she calls from the highest point of the city.*

*"Let all who are simple come in here!"*
  *she says to those who lack judgment.*
*"Come eat my food and drink the wine I have mixed.*
  *Leave your simple ways and you will live;*
  *walk in the way of understanding.*
*The fear of the LORD is the beginning of wisdom,*
  *and knowledge of the Holy One is understanding.*
*For through me your days will be many,*
  *and years will be added to your life."*

The woman Folly is loud;
   she is undisciplined and without knowledge.
She sits at the door of her house,
   on a seat at the highest point of the city,
calling out to those who pass by,
   who go straight on their way.

"Let all who are simple come in here!"
   she says to those who lack judgment.
"Stolen water is sweet;
   food eaten in secret is delicious!"
But little do they know that the dead are there,
   that her guests are in the depths of the grave.

If you are wise, your wisdom will reward you;
   if you are a mocker, you alone will suffer.

# Reading twenty-nine

A scoundrel and villain, who goes about with a corrupt mouth,
  who winks with his eye, signals with his feet
  and motions with his fingers,
who plots evil with deceit in his heart—
  he always stirs up dissension.
Therefore disaster will overtake him in an instant;
  he will suddenly be destroyed—without remedy.

There are six things the LORD hates,
  seven that are detestable to him:
    haughty eyes,
    a lying tongue,
    hands that shed innocent blood,
    a heart that devises wicked schemes,
    feet that are quick to rush into evil,
    a false witness who pours out lies
    and a man who stirs up dissension among brothers.

Go to the ant, you sluggard;
   consider its ways and be wise!
It has no commander,
   no overseer or ruler,
yet it stores its provisions in summer
   and gathers its food at harvest.

How long will you lie there, you sluggard?
   When will you get up from your sleep?
A little sleep, a little slumber,
   a little folding of the hands to rest—
and poverty will come on you like a bandit
   and scarcity like an armed man.

# Reading thirty

*Wisdom will save you from the ways of wicked men,*
  *from men whose words are perverse,*
*who leave the straight paths*
  *to walk in dark ways,*
*who delight in doing wrong*
  *and rejoice in the perverseness of evil.*

*It will save you also from the adulteress,*
  *from the wayward wife with her seductive words,*
*who has left the partner of her youth*
  *and ignored the covenant she made before God.*

*He holds victory in store for the upright,*
  *he is a shield to those whose walk is blameless,*
*for he guards the course of the just*
  *and protects the way of his faithful ones.*

*Thus you will walk in the ways of good men*
   *and keep to the paths of the righteous.*
*My son, if you accept my words*
   *and store up my commands within you,*
*turning your ear to wisdom*
   *and applying your heart to understanding,*
*and if you look for it as for silver*
   *and search for it as for hidden treasure,*
*then you will understand the fear of the LORD*
   *and find the knowledge of God.*

*Then you will understand what is right*
   *and just and fair—every good path.*
*For wisdom will enter your heart,*
   *and knowledge will be pleasant to your soul.*
*Discretion will protect you,*
   *and understanding will guard you.*

*Surely you desire truth in the inner parts;*
*you teach me wisdom in the inmost*
*place.*